Finding Personal Success:
Knowing Yourself

BY

Doug Ross

Finding Personal Success:
Knowing Yourself

Doug Ross, Ph.D.

ISBN 9781466375048
First Edition 2008
Second Edition 2010
Third Edition 2011
Fourth Edition 2012
Fifth Edition 2014

$4.99

Screen Beans are from
A Bit Better Corporation
www.bitbetter.com

Doug Ross, Ph.D.
Sarasota, Florida
www.doug-ross.com

Contents

THIS BOOK

This book is a compilation of advice that will help you be a happier, more successful person, and this advice is yours to take or leave. Nobody can make you do anything unless you want to do it. It is a very old saying, but still very true, "You can lead a horse to water, but you can't make it drink!"

Finding Personal Success

Doug Ross

These wisdoms, tips, or steps, were collected from many sources. The original *47 Steps to Being Who You Are* immediately follow the newer collections, and when you encounter a seemingly repeated suggestion, know that I intended it to be so.

We all want success. We want it in our personal lives and in our businesses and work lives. These collected wisdoms will help reach that mountaintop.

In this 5th edition, I continue moving in the direction of looking inside to better know the self. In this edition I summarize Steven Covey's "Seven Habits . . ." and John C. Maxwell's "How Successful People Think" and add my own self assessment.

The bullet approach allows for a fast read, but some of these wisdoms are worth contemplating longer. What if you choose one to work on each day? There are enough here for five months.

You are welcome to add some of your own wisdoms!

How to Know Yourself

To know who you want to be, you have to know yourself as you are now. None of us are perfect, or we don't even really know what perfect means when asking about ourselves. People don't stop and remain fixed in stone. We keep evolving; we keep learning; we keep adjusting to the ever changing environment around us. So we ask who we are now, and what is the gap to being what we want to become?

How many ways are there to know who we are? When looking in the mirror we see what we *look* like. We can ask our families who they *think* we are. We can ask friends, business associates, teachers, mentors, colleagues, and even some people who have just met us. The more ways we try to find out who other people think we are, the more we can discern whether they see us as we see ourselves.

One exercise to try goes like this:

Make a list of 15 – 20 people who know you. Send them a letter (or an email, text, or tweet) is easiest these days). In it ask them to say what they think are your best qualities. Suggest they find from 5 to 10 qualities. Don't lead them in any way.

Tell them you are doing a self assessment and that you will use it to create a unique selling proposition (USP) for your business hopes and plans. Ask them to do this right away, and give them a deadline at the end of the week. Maybe say that you are working on a resume update. Think of how you could urge them to respond.

When you get the responses, and 8 – 10 would be enough, look at what they said and see what items repeat, or we could say, see what they all agree on about you. Respond by thanking them for helping you. Later, you may want to get some feedback from those you trust and respect most when the whole list is in, but for now, let them know you are happy to have received their perspectives.

There are still other ways to learn about yourself. There are "self assessment" instruments you can access to add to what your colleagues and friends have generated. One of the most popular, well known, and respected instruments is the Myers-Briggs Type Inventory (MBTI). You will probably either need to pay a professional to administer it to you or pay for the instrument. If you Google "Self Assessment" and Myers-Briggs, you'll also be able to find out how to use it. Many businesses use the

MBTI in hiring and for other personnel functions, so an HR Department may be able to help you. Counselors and Therapists also often use the Myers-Briggs to quickly learn about their clients.

There are other similar devices, e.g., The Big Five Personality Dimensions, DISC, Four Colors, and a favorite of mine, The Kolbe. You can find each by using Google. The Kolbe gives you feedback in more detail than many of the others, and can suggest best matches with positions you are well suited to hold in the business world. No matter which instrument you decide to use, be as honest as possible in responding. Doing it is for you to learn more about yourself!

What do I do with this information?

Finding out more about who you are empowers you to be authentic in all your interactions and engagements. When you know who you are, others can't lead you into ideas or places you know don't work for you. You can avoid being with negative people who only seem to want to tear you down. You can know that no matter where you are and what you are doing, when it is over you will still be exactly who you are on your way to being precisely who you really want to be.

9

You will also discover that you can change for the better. These instruments are for you to be with yourself. You can choose whether to change or not. You can allow yourself to be better. You can strive to reach higher goals. You will begin to realize that others can't manipulate you, or get you to do anything that is false or unlike the reality you now know about yourself.

You will be stronger in every relationship, not strong meaning you will always try to win at another's loss, but strong in staying true to yourself. Be honest, truthful, and open to hear other points of view. Be able to hear others that you didn't think you could ever agree with and seek to "stand in the other person's moccasins". You'll discover you can be a great listener.

[I have shared my own assessment of myself in the "Afterthoughts" of this book.]

~~~~~~~~

ON CIVILITY:
TEN PLUS ONE POINTS OF CIVILITY

Respect others - Honor other's ideas,
even when they differ from yours

Think Positively - Keep and open mind
and assume others have good intentions

Pay Attention - Be aware of and attend to
the world and people around you

Make a difference - Get involved in something
that has meaning for you

Speak kindly - Choose not to spread or listen to
gossip about others

Say 'thank you" - Let others know you appreciate
them and what they do

Accept others - Our differences make us interesting

Rediscover silence - Keep noise to a minimum

Listen - Focus on others who are speaking to better
understand their point of view

Speak softly and respectfully - Give your point of
view without arguing for it

Keep your cool - Accept life's challenges with grace

11

On Beliefs

If your life feels like you are trapped in a prison of limitations, or you're just not living up to your full potential, chances are you have a conflict between your **conscious desires** and your **subconscious beliefs**. This kind of conflict shows up in relationships, self esteem, spirituality, health, prosperity, personal power, grief, and your body including weight loss and other disorders

" . . . . rewrite the software of your mind in order to change the printout of your life!"
Rob Williams - Psych-K

Part One: How to Be

The word BE is important here because it doesn't mean "try to work toward". It is how you need to act and think every day and all the time. Many of these ways "to be" are learned by what happens when you aren't "being" this way. We learn most from our mistakes, and then we need to change how we act and not revert.

Why is it useful to be any certain way? Aren't we already whatever we are? In business, and I dare say, in personal life as well, we usually want to matter, to have some skin in the game, to influence how our work or life will bring us satisfaction and joy. How we are, how real we are, how open and honest we can be with others, how consistent we are within ourselves, the more people will trust us and allow us to influence them. So this little book of wisdom is about not just being who you are, but Finding Personal Success!

1.   Be Punctual: It is far better to be early and prepared, than to dash in to the office at the last minute and feel rushed all day.

2.   Look good: Dress for success is always best. If you dress well you will feel well. You never get a second chance to make a first impression on others. Your appearance alone speaks volumes. If people visit your office, keep it neat and clean. It is another way you become known.

3.   Show up: Always get to work on time so you do not overburden your colleague or your superiors. If you can't make it or will be late, call on the phone to let them know.

4.   Be Reliable: The boss needs to know he or she can count on you. So does your spouse or significant other.

5. **Be Honest:** Honesty is always the best policy. If you cannot be trusted you have nothing. With trust comes potential influence.

6. **Be Clean:** It is said that "Cleanliness is next to Godliness". You must be clean and dressed appropriately for your workplace. Your dress and demeanor are both non-verbal clues to who you are and what you stand for.

7. **Be Respectful:** You might not always agree with everyone but you benefit from respecting their feelings and knowledge.

8. **Be Cooperative:** Everyone likes a team player. It doesn't mean everybody has to be your best friend, but it pays to find a way to work together.

9.   Be Prepared: Do everything in a timely and concise manner, it is far better to be ahead of the game than to constantly be playing catch up. Prioritize.

10.   Be Consistent: Consistency always leads to predictability and everyone loves dependability. Consistency doesn't mean you can't improve, however!

11.   Have an Open Mind: Always be open to new and creative ideas. You don't have to appropriate all of them, but in the world of ideas, different is good!

12.   Be Flexible: Learn to be able to adapt to new ways and change things mid-stream if the need arises. Sometimes it helps to put in some added hours and not be committed to a rigid schedule.

13. **Be Resourceful:** Be aware of different ways to do things, to the results of research, and to open mindedness. You may not know how to do something, but you should know how to find out *how* to do it. Try Google's You Tube.

14. **Stay Current:** Make sure you keep your ideas and technology up to date. Constantly learn what is new in your field. Be knowledgeable of current events in the world as well. It helps to keep crucial conversations flowing easily.

.

15. **Be Strong:** Stand up for yourself. Do not let yourself get walked on, but be respectful of others.

16. **Be Balanced:** You must be strong AND flexible.

17.   Treat others as you want to be treated: It goes back to the Golden Rule – "do unto others as you would have them do unto you."

18.   Don't Judge A Book By its Cover: Look deeper into people and do not assume anything. Ask open ended questions. Give everyone and everything a chance.

19.   Be A Good Listener: Take time to listen and you may learn something new and important. People like to know that you are truly listening to what they have to say. Hearing someone's words does not necessarily mean that you are listening. Summarize and paraphrase what they have said. They will feel heard.

20.   Be Down To Earth: Be a real person – just be yourself, have no airs about you, let people know who you are.

21.   Have Realistic Expectations: Try to avoid preconceived expectations and don't hold everyone, including yourself, up to those notions.

22.   Be Professional: A professional code is expected in business. Think before you speak or act. You always need to keep your cool; don't lose your temper; think before you speak ("Look before you leap").

23.   Work To Live, and don't Live To Work: You must keep a good balance in your life. It can't be only work, or all play. Good work provides good self esteem, and that improves the rest of your life.

24.   Have an Outlet: You must have a way to unwind from a hectic schedule, find a hobby or activity you enjoy and pursue it.

25.   Keep Personal Matters At Home: When you walk in the door at work, your attention should be there and there alone; personal and family life issues should be left at the door.

26. Think Outside The Box: Be innovative and have fresh ideas, keep an open mind.

27. Be Culturally Aware: If you are dealing with multi-cultural people, remember that different customs apply. Be aware and alert to those so you do not offend anyone. Take time to do research so you know.

28. Be Passionate: Successful leaders have a passion and are willing to do what it takes to fulfill that passion. When you are passionate about something, it shows and is admired and respected in the eyes of others.

29. Appreciate: Be appreciative of people and things; never take anything for granted, or it could be lost. Tell people what you like about them and their work.

30. Be Positive: Negativity never gains anything. If you have a positive attitude things just go better. People like to be around positive people.

31. Be Energetic: High energy is contagious; if you are motivated and energetic, all of your co-workers will be also.

32. Give Eye Contact: Always maintain eye contact with the people you speak with. It gives them a sense of your knowledge, your trustworthiness, and a general good feeling. Nod and smile; both say you hear them.

33. Be Polite: Always mind your manners and be respectful to people you are with or that are around you. You never know when you will see someone again or how you will be remembered? Burn no bridges.

34. Be Organized: If you have good organizational skills, you will be much more productive and accomplish more. If you aren't, start with a time management course and structure your space so you can   work effectively.

35.   Admit When You Are Wrong: Everyone makes mistakes but it takes a big person to admit it and apologize. We do learn from our mistakes, so the key is not to repeat them! Don't dwell on your mistakes and become a "poor me" victim. Move on.

36.   Have A Goal: Reach for the stars and keep reaching. We all must have something to strive for. That something, whatever it may be, is what keeps us motivated and alive. In business, have a vision of a rewarding and successful future.

37.   Strive To Learn: We are never too old to learn; it's fun and makes us better people.

38.   Smile: A smile can win over anyone and anything. It makes everyone feel better, even ourselves. There are 40 muscles in our faces involved in smiling, and it is almost impossible to smile and feel lousy!

39. **Be Compassionate:** Always consider the other person whether it is a co-worker or a boss. Put yourself in their shoes and see how comfortable you might be.

40. **Be patient**: Some very positive outcomes take time to unfold. You can't "push a rope". Sometimes you just need to stop and think. Reflect on your day, your week, your life. Refocus on success and happiness, and allow your choices to unfold.

Part Two: Covey's *Seven Habits* and Maxwell's *Successful Thinking*

Covey's Seven Habits

Independence or Self-Mastery

The First Three Habits surround moving from dependence to independence (i.e., self-mastery):

- **Habit 1: Be Proactive**

Take initiative in life by realizing that your decisions (and how they align with life's principles) are the primary determining factor for effectiveness in your life. Take responsibility for your choices and the consequences that follow.

- **Habit 2: Begin with the End in Mind**

Self-discover and clarify your deeply important character values and life goals. Envision the ideal characteristics for each of your various roles and relationships in life. Create a mission statement.

- **Habit 3: Put First Things First**

Prioritize, plan, and execute your week's tasks based on importance rather than urgency. Evaluate whether your efforts exemplify your desired character values, propel you toward goals, and enrich the roles and relationships that were elaborated in Habit 2.

Interdependence

The next three have to do with Interdependence (i.e., working with others):

- **Habit 4: Think Win-Win**

Genuinely strive for mutually beneficial solutions or agreements in your relationships. Value and respect people by understanding a "win" for all is ultimately a better long-term resolution than if only one person in the situation had gotten his way.

- **Habit 5: Seek First to Understand, Then to be Understood**

Use empathic listening to be genuinely influenced by a person, which compels them to reciprocate the listening and take an open mind to being influenced by you. This creates an atmosphere of caring, respect, and positive problem solving.

- **Habit 6: Synergize**

Combine the strengths of people through positive teamwork, so as to achieve goals no one person could have done alone.

Self Renewal

The Last habit relates to self-rejuvenation:

- **Habit 7: Sharpen the Saw**

Balance and renew your resources, energy, and health to create a sustainable, long-term, effective lifestyle. It primarily emphasizes exercise for physical renewal, prayer (meditation, yoga, etc.) and good reading for mental renewal. It also mentions service to society for spiritual renewal.

Habit 8: Effectiveness

Effectiveness does not suffice in "The Knowledge Worker Age". The challenges and complexity we face today are of a different order of magnitude. "Find your voice and inspire others to find theirs..."

~~~~~

Maxwell's 11 Ways of Thinking

1. **Big Picture Thinking** - "You have to think anyway, so why not think big?" "Big picture thinking allows you to lead." **"Am I thinking beyond myself and my world so that I possess ideas with a holistic perspective?"**

2. **Focused Thinking** - Knowledge is power only if a man (sic) knows what not to bother about." "Be willing to give up some things you love in order to focus on what has the greatest impact." **"Am I dedicated to removing distractions and mental clutter so that I can concentrate with clarity on the real issue?"**

3. **Creative Thinking** - "The most valuable resource you bring to your work and to your firm is your creativity." "Personally, I would sooner have written *Alice in Wonderland* than the whole *Encyclopedia Britannica*." **"Am I working to break out of my "box" of limitations so that I can**

explore ideas and options to experience creative breakthroughs?"

4. Realistic Thinking - Ruckert's Law - Believing there is nothing so small that it can't be blown out of proportion." "The truth will set you free, but first it will make you angry" **"Am I building a solid mental foundation on facts so that I can think with certainty?"**

5. **Strategic Thinking** -"Most people spend more time planning their summer vacation than planning their lives." "Successful generals make plans to fit circumstances, but do not try to create circumstances to fit plans." "Nothing is particularly hard if you divide it into small jobs." **"Am I implementing strategic plans that give me direction for today and increase my potential for tomorrow ?"**

6. **Possibility Thinking** - "Big thinkers are in creating positive forward-looking optimistic pictures in their own minds and in the minds of others." "Make your plans as fantastic as you like,

because twenty-five years from now they will seem mediocre." **"Am I unleashing the enthusiasm of possibility thinking to find solutions for even seemingly impossible situations?"**

7. **Reflective Thinking** - "Reflective thinking enables you to distance yourself from the intense emotions of particularly good or bad experiences and see them with *fresh eyes*." "Ultimately, reflective thinking has three main values: it gives perspective within context; it allows one to connect with *one's journey;* and it provides counsel and direction concerning the future." **"Am I regularly revisiting the past to gain perspective and think with understanding?"**

8. **Popular Thinking** - Question the acceptance. "The difficulty lies not so much in developing new ideas as escaping from the old ones!" The problem with popular thinking is that it doesn't require you to think at all!" **"Am I consciously rejecting the**

limitations of common thinking in order to accomplish uncommon results?"

9. **Shared Thinking** - "We live in a truly fast-paced world. To function at its current rate of speed, we can't go it alone." "None of us is as smart as all of us." "Listening to advice often accomplishes far more than heeding it." **"Am I consistently including the heads of others to think "over my head" and achieve compounding results?"**

10. **Unselfish Thinking** - Unselfish Thinking - "We cannot hold a torch to light another's path without brightening our own." "Getters generally don't *get* happiness; givers get it." "People with humility don't think less of themselves; they just think of themselves less." **"Am I continually considering others and their journey in order to think with maximum collaboration?**

11. Bottom-Line Thinking - "We keep asking ourselves very simple questions, "What is our business? Who are our customers? And, what does the customer consider of value?" "We try never to forget that medicine is for the people. It is not for the profits. The profits follow, and if we remember that, they have never failed to appear." **"Am I staying focused on the bottom line so that I can gain the maximum return and reap the full potentiality of my thinking?"**

More to Ponder

- You only have one chance to make a first impression!
- Don't just think outside the box. There is no box!
- Your attitude is a choice. Be positive.
- When you are wrong, take responsibility for it.
- Integrity is built through trust.
- Collaborate.
- Look for improvables.
- Take 24 hours to make big decisions.

- There are two (or more) sides to every story. Look for the other sides.
- If you have a complaint, offer a solution.
- If you are feeling down, keep it to yourself, or share it with a very close friend.
- Don't worry about things beyond your control.
- Make best risk decisions.
- Say "please" and "thank you".
- Don't one-up your friend's story.
- Record a positive and upbeat voicemail message.
- When necessary, apologize and mean it.
- Identify your strengths and passions and combine them with your resources.
- Think like an entrepreneur. Market yourself honestly and well.
- Be financially responsible. Budget.
- Balance work and family life and combine your priorities.
- Lead in tough times by being steady; be open to opportunities.
- Lead by example.
- "It's not whether you win or lose. It's how you play the game."

- To win, if necessary, persist. Remember the tortoise!
- Be punctual, and if somebody is waiting for you, call them to say you are delayed.

PART THREE: MORE WAYS TO SUCCESS

In addition to what we learn from mistakes, we can learn by watching what other successful people do and say. Here is some wisdom from some respected thinkers.

1.   Be Proactive and not always reactive (Covey): Surf the front of the wave and avoid the wash.

2.   Sharpen the saw (Covey): The tree won't fall if you use a dull saw blade. Hone your skills.

3.   Preserve the Core; Stimulate Progress (Porras and Collins): Find what is always true for you in any enterprise, and stick to it. At the same time, find new ways to stay current and competitive.

4.   Use "Both – and" Thinking: Many are stuck with "either – or" thinking. Everything is black or white. Try to see the grey areas.

5.   "No" isn't the last word! Ask for what you want, but don't be attached to outcomes, and if you get a "no" answer, wait and see if any alternatives are offered. Most of the time, a pretty good deal, even a better one, follows the "No".

6.   Set Audacious Goals (Porras and Collins): Big Hairy Audacious Goals (BHAG) can be reached. Even better, set a tone for all those around you. If you never imagine it, you'll never get it.

7.   Be a Leader: The definition of a leader is that there are followers. Lead yourself. Realize that others will watch what you do and copy you. Be a great model.

8.   Trust brings Influence: The best leaders are trusted and respected. These qualities allow followers to be influenced. You won't influence anybody who doesn't trust you.

9.   It is better to delegate some of your work than to die on the job! Delegation skills can be learned, and it also takes time for the delegee to learn your ways of doing things. Communicate your needs carefully. They will make some mistakes. Take the long view of benefits to you. Go slow to go fast!

10.   Embrace Change: Don't fight change. It is everywhere.

11.   Think Clearly: "In this day and age, if you are not confused, you are not thinking clearly." (Burt Nanus) Regardless of what Burt says, think clearly.

12. **"Organizations can change only at the pace at which the values and abilities of the people within the organization change."** (Cameron and Vanderwoerd)

13. **Who is on your bus?** "Get the right people on the bus, the wrong people off the bus, and get the people in the right seats." (Collins) The hiring process is crucial to business success, and the skill of finding other work for those who don't fit is equally crucial. Who you choose to be with in your private life also influences your success.

14. **Are you on the right bus?** Make sure you fit your job, your family, and the culture of your organization. You'll be unhappy and perform less than well if you are in the wrong job or marriage!

15. **Beware of the Status Quo!** Complacency is numbing. Keep seeking new and better ways of working. Be a learning member of a learning organization.

16.   Where you are going? Casey Stengel, long time manager of the New York Yankees baseball team said, "If you don't know where you are going, you may end up somewhere else." Make a plan and a backup plan.

17.   Asking for the hard questions: Successful leaders urge their followers to ask them the hard questions. This works in personal life as well. Welcome differences in point of view, and then decide whether you want or need to change.

18.   Implementing Change: The hardest thing about plans to change is implementing the plan. The only solution is to do the change over and over again. It takes many repetitions to balance out an old and well established habit, and many more to establish the new habit. "Plan your work, and work your plan", and then revisit it.

19. **More on Change:** Nobody plans to fail, but many fail to plan. If you do what you've always done, you'll get what you've always gotten. Think outside of the box.

20. **Style is no substitute for substance:** You have to be who you are. "Walk your talk", be knowledgeable, honest, and forthright. People will respect you and want you to lead.

21. **Egocentricity:** The wise leader keeps egocentricity in check and by doing so becomes more effective.

22. **Take time to Reflect:** Allow time for silent reflection. Turn inward and digest what has happened. Reflection is a growing practice in consolidation of our memory. Brain research shows that memory consolidates over a 24 – 48 hour time period.

23. **Opportunity:** People need opportunities to grow. We can be open to opportunities, but take only very few. The key is to see the possibilities, and sense the ones that will lead to satisfaction and success. Be broad and vigilant rather than narrow. Be awake and conscious of what you are doing.

24. **Self Awareness:** Who are we really? Learn about who you are. Learn from tests, from evaluations, from your family and friends. You have to want to know and you have to ask for feedback. Ask for your "plusses". Don't ask for your flaws, but rather seek your "improvables". It feels better that way and is easier to embrace. (See

25. **Be Engaged** : Get involved in what is going on around you. Make contributions. Be on the team, and not always an outside observer. Work actively toward your goals and the goals of your organization. If they conflict, get off the bus.

26.   Attitude Matters: Attitude toward life, toward yourself, and toward others makes a huge difference in what you attract back to yourself.

27.   Inspiration: Breathe in the spirit! Inspired people have the spirit within themselves, and it aims them at high values and success. You inspire others by being a model.

28.   What you really want: The universe is there, and has whatever is wanted by you. You really have to want it; it is not sufficient to just say it but not believe. "You gotta believe!"
Tug McGraw, Phillies relief pitcher.

29.   Do it: Sometimes we read about something that will improve us, or we hear a lecture or attend an inspirational talk. If you want to be better, take action on the new idea. Do it!

30. Persevere: Many successful entrepreneurs have had to restart their plans many times before they got it right. If you have a great idea, persevere in putting it into action. The commitment pays off.

31. Success often comes out of what we learn from failure. When you make a mistake, take responsibility, and then make a permanent change so you never make that mistake again.

32. Pay attention to what grabs your interest. Notice when you sit up straighter, when you are leaning in, when you know you want to say something, when your eyes widen and your ears perk up. What makes you stop whatever else you are doing to attend to the new?

33. Creativity time: When we are sleeping our brains are at rest, ideas that aren't heard with all the noise of life, finally get to the surface. Write these ideas down. If you don't, they may be gone when you wake up tomorrow.

34.   Work on your business, not in your business: Hire somebody to do repetitive tasks so you have time to plan to think. (Gerber)

35.   Be present: Wherever you are and whatever you are doing, show up. Engage.

36.   Persevere: Have stamina. It is amazing how working steadily generates results. When you think you've reached your limit, do one more thing.

37.   Focus on the benefits of what you do. Do what matters.

38.   Look for people with interests like your own. Is there something you could do as partners that would be helpful to both of you.

39.   Don't be afraid to ask for help, even if you think you have the answer or can do it alone. You don't know everything.

40.   Identify Your Definite Purpose:
(Napoleon Hill) Set a goal and a time to reach it. Collect friends and colleagues to be your Master-Mind Group that will help you and remind you of your commitment.

41.   Smile ☺ Present yourself well at every opportunity. Give "World Class" customer service.

42.   Compassion: If you want others to be happy, practice compassion. If *you* want to be happy, practice compassion. (Dalai Lama)

43.   Luck: Remember that not getting what you want is sometimes a wonderful stroke of luck. (Dalai Lama)

44.   Communicate, Communicate!

a.   Say what you have to say succinctly, i.e., don't go on and on and repeat it over again

b.   Keep on target; don't wander off into loosely related topics

c.   Look at the person with whom you are speaking

d.   Listen to what others are saying in such a way that you could reflect it back to them accurately. Reflect it back so they know you heard them correctly.

e.   Listen actively: nod, look at the speaker, be interested, try to hear from the other person's point of view

f.   Don't interrupt.

g.   Don't start preparing what you are going to say while they are still speaking to you

h.   In groups, listen for the "sense" of what the group is thinking.

i.   Be aware of your non-verbals: What is your face saying? Your posture? How you dressed?

j.   What are you communicating by the way you keep your office or house? How you decorate your office? Your wall hangings, furniture, carpeting?

PART FOUR : The Original 47 Steps
(Author House, 2006)

1. Find out who you are; who have you been?
Who are you now? Who will you be? Most of
us don't know how to ask for feedback about
ourselves. Maybe we don't want to hear some
truths. Business leaders have consultants
interview stakeholders and then give feedback to
the company so it can better itself. People need
to do this too. Who are the stakeholders in your
life? Who do they say you are?

2. Be honest and realistic. Be truthful and
sensitive, but be sure to be grounded and in
touch with reality. The safest way to be honest
is to say how you are feeling. The reason for
this is that feelings are inside of us. As soon as
we say what or who is the cause, there is a good
chance that person will feel blamed, so say how
you feel and describe the situation that
generated the feeling. Being honest is
sometimes difficult for others to hear, but if it is
an important truth, the longer term outcome will
be better.

3. Be idealistic; strive for quality in all you do. Seek the highest ground. Don't settle for good enough, do what it takes to be better. The quality movement in business came about because U.S. companies were not matching the quality of products from Japan and Germany and were losing market share. If you want to keep your market share, do it well the first time. Make it a practice to make excellent products and provide quality service.

4. Treat people well, with courtesy, respect, and caring. Appreciate and honor others. Never be rude, disrespectful, overbearing, unkind, or hostile. Try to understand that people are different, have different values, come from different cultures, have different beliefs. Let it be acceptable to be different.

5. Be grounded, down to earth, straight forward, and authentic. Don't be haughty, and lord it over people. Don't use jargon or pseudo-sophisticated language to attempt to appear better than somebody else. Don't be obtuse; talk straight and stay on the point without wandering off. Be real; be who you really are and be comfortable with who you really are. Businesses identify and publicize their life force and organizing principles to remain clearly focused. They create missions, visions, and values lists and revisit their purposes. You can do that too.

6. When you are working with another person or a group, get agreement on purpose. Take time up front to find out if you are in agreement, and try to work toward joint purpose. Revisit purpose often. See if you both still agree. If it seems like it is unclear, ask, "We are doing this because . . . ?'

7. Agree on a meaningful mission - one that has heart and soul in it. Whether at work or thinking of your own life, write a mission statement and live by it. Find a way to make your work and personal life meaningful so that you can look back and be proud of yourself. Be sure the mission you write or speak is the mission you live and believe.

8. Especially in business, but in family relationships too, have a clear shared vision. Be sure it is really shared. This means everybody has an equal role in its creation and will work to make it work. For a flexible shared vision, have scenarios, or backup plans for most eventualities you can imagine. Have alternative plans of action depending on what happens beyond your control.

9. See that your world is changing; ask what risks you are willing to take to keep up with the changes. Change is always with us, inside of us, in our relationships and partnerships, and in the groups we work in. Change is happening around us, whether we like it or not. It is better to surf the front of the wave than be caught in the wash. Embrace change. Take risks that will make change easy for you.

10. Listen attentively to what people are saying. Be open to their ideas. Seek diverse opinions. Do this so that it is second nature to understand that we all are different, and that no one is big enough to know it all. Others' ideas can add to your own. Ask them what they think. Diversity generates creativity, because we are forced to see things in new and different ways. Embrace diversity.

11. Speak from a deep place of wisdom. Trust yourself more than regurgitating what others have said. Filter knowledge through your experience and speak from that wisdom. Get in touch with what things mean to you. This is a way to know who you are. Don't brag, or make promises you can't keep. Find common ground among those you are with. Ask how we are similar; "what do we have in common?"

12. Ask questions that expand possibilities. Invite in more than you know or have said. Be interested in another person's view. Ask how we can make this better. Ask what other reference point would add to what we are thinking about now. Ask questions that begin with, "What if . . . ?"

13. Encourage creativity. Generate ideas and let them incubate. Try an idea that seems unrelated at first; see whether it adds to the thinking. Invite in the new, the unusual, and the different. Rearrange your furniture in a uniquely different way and try it out. You can always to return to the old way if it was better.

14. Own your truth and speak it without judging others. Be honest, and be sure you mean what you say. Judgments are born out of needs to be right, to be better than, or more of, or higher than. What if there is no right or wrong, but only what is. What can we learn from differences? Rumi said, "Out beyond wrongdoing and rightdoing, there is a field. I'll meet you there." Meet me in that field.

15. Pay attention to what energizes you. These things are your passion, and you will be easily motivated to engage and do well. If you seem to have no passion in your life or work, please go sit in the warm sun and ask the warmth to raise your passion so you can see it. Ask others what they think you love. What lights up your eyes? What makes you sit on the edge of your seat? What stops you when you are walking past? Get involved in these things to make your life more meaningful.

16. Let go of your pet ideas if others don't like them. Don't always argue to win. We sometimes get caught up in ourselves and think it is important to have the best idea, or the wisest thing to say. We are posturing. Try saying what you think and letting go of the outcome. If others like it, it will be embraced. If they don't, let go. Maybe this is not the time, or the place. Try it again later, or with different people. Find the "win" in what we all want.

17. Appreciate what people do, including you. You can't be appreciated too much if it is authentic. Watch for things people do that you like and compliment them. Notice that you too are worth appreciating. Maybe you need to appreciate yourself to appreciate others. Make a list for yourself of things you appreciate about yourself. Be specific; point out details of your appreciation.

18. Be willing to be passionate when something matters to you. Emotions are a good thing; don't hide them. Find out if you can be passionate and still willing to let go if your idea isn't embraced. You will feel good about yourself for having authentically expressed what is important for you. Be sure to remember to "do no harm".

19. Think of your system. This means don't be narrow-minded. In a business, there are many factors working at once, suppliers, contacts, past reputation, personal relations, visions, internal and external environments, customers, distribution, laws and much, much more. Personal lives are influenced in many ways. Our bodies are themselves complex systems, with rhythms, shapes, strengths and weakness, and a huge variety of states of mind. Open up to all that is around you and how these diverse factors influence you or your business.

20. Give gifts. Small or large, gifts make people happy. Some of your gifts are human gifts, as in the services you provide, and deep listening, or experiences you can share. Companies give to their communities, give to their employees, contribute to a better world. Give to your self. Make your world better.

21. Don't give up doing what you do best. Think all the way back to your childhood and think about two or three things you have always been good at. Keep doing these things. If you change jobs, move, enter a new relationship, keep doing what you do well and work to improve it. These are your real gifts.

22. "Understand and then seek to be understood." Stephen Covey said this in The Seven Habits of Highly Effective People. What good advice! Listen well and ask questions. If you demonstrate your interest in other people, they will be interested in you! If they are not, you may not be destined to be friends.

23. Plan your work; work your plan. Planning prepares you and makes the way easier to traverse. Implementing it will be easier, even if the plan needs to be revised in mid-course. Some businesses are using scenario planning to generate more than one plan. This is necessary since we don't always know what the future holds for us.

24. Give up rightness and wrongness. Why is it so important to be right? Who cares if somebody thinks differently than us. What if we recall things differently? A key to emerge from these questions is, "Can we agree to disagree?" "There are many ways to skin a cat", a gruesome expression, but a valid one. My friend Jim Long used to say that there are three ways to do anything, the right way, the wrong way, and the Long way!

25. Seek a long-term view. Lift your head and see the horizon. Long views offer more perspective, and sometimes indicate the vastness of the terrain. Long views are valuable to companies who want to stay viable in an extended future fraught with change. Short-term thinking causes trouble. Do you have a quarterly bottom line? Does it keep you thinking about the short run? Stand along an ocean, or on a mountaintop and look out and up. Stand on the brink of the Grand Canyon. Listen to what you are thinking.

26. Mourn losses; then move on. Loss will happen to all of us. It is worth grieving, letting ourselves fully experience what was and is no more. Tears are healthy ways to wash the face. If one grieves a loss and allows the emotions to flow, it is easier to move on. Don't wallow in pain. Wallowing is not moving on. Some of us like to wallow. Why does that feel good? There is an answer. All that we do can be understood as serving our needs in some way.

27. Stay away from negative thinkers. Positive thinking may lead to better outcomes for a number of reasons, but what seems most clear, is that negative thinking stymies good action. People who go around with the attitude that nothing good can happen create self-fulfilling prophecies. Believing we can meet our objectives, that our best visions are possible, that our health is improved by our attitude, or that we can reach our ideals, creates an aura of confidence. Actions follow from our thoughts.

28. Build buffers into your life. Buffers are quiet moments between tasks or actions. These moments allow us to reset ourselves, to renew our plan, to make a check of our intentions, and to allow us to breathe. We live in a fast paced world, and busy workers and parents often move stressfully from one thing to another without stopping. Buffers give us pause to reflect. Buffers let us notice the beauty of our world, enjoy and appreciate people, and get us in touch with our souls.

29. Make a list of values and update them every month. Live by them every day. Values guide us. They help us make choices, and formulate important decisions. In a complex society, opportunity provides for satisfaction of our values, or presents new opportunities. By framing a new set of values monthly, we can both reaffirm our ongoing commitments and open up to new possibilities. Post your values someplace where you can see the list everyday to remind you of what is important to you.

30. Stand back, get the whole picture, a larger view. Use the opportunity to examine the internal and external environment you live in. In business there is often a need for a retreat. Retreats are used to build community, to plan, to vision, and to get together in different places with different people than is normally the case. Individuals can also go on retreats, to a beautiful place, a mountain, to a babbling brook in a deep wood, to the oceans, lakes and parks that surround us. The big picture lets us stop and access where we are and where we are going next.

31. Arrange for silence and reflection in your life and work. Reflection is a time to take stock, to assess the past and imagine the future. Many workplaces are noisy and busy. Try to find a rooftop, a quiet corner, a soft chair. Advocate for a silent room where people meditate or rest. At home, turn off the TV set and all music and appliances for five minutes. Create a silent moment in your life and love it.

32. Know what you want and ask for it, but don't be attached to getting it! Asking for what we want is a gift to others. Their guesses about us are destined to be wrong much of the time. Something interesting happens when we ask for what we want. Be careful what you ask for! Sometimes the answer will be "No". But notice, it is hard to just stop with "No". Something usually follows "No", and sometimes it is actually better than what you asked for, so put it out there, but be careful not to be attached to outcome, at least not right away.

33. Say what you mean; do what you say. This comes from Martin Buber by way of Angeles Arrien. When not upheld, it is the single best predictor of conflict in the world. Make the commitment today, and take it one day at a time. Think before you agree to do anything, and only agree if you know you can carry out the commitment.

34. After you think you have done what you can, do a little more. After you've done your best, see if you can do a little better. You'll be surprised.

35. Listen to children. Smell the roses. While innocence is our heritage, we do have to learn to protect and defend ourselves. The rose is vulnerable to all sorts of destruction, so see it, smell it, touch it. Notice its pure uniqueness, the vividness of colors. The pure innocence of the child lives in each of us.

36. Love your mother. You couldn't have gotten here without her

Finding Personal Success

37. "Chop wood; carry water." For Ram Dass this meant live your life in the present. Do the simple things that please you and others. Pay attention to these humble tasks. Enjoy life. "Be here, now."

38. "Follow your bliss." Joseph Campbell adds to the simplicity of staying present. Do what matters to you. Get in touch with what you love, and be that.

39. "There are a thousand ways to kneel and kiss
the Earth." Rumi asks us to find love and
enjoyment inside ourselves. Examine your habits.
Are you living on autopilot? Write a poem
today. Play the dulcimer. Do what you love to do.

40. "The greatest gift we can give to anyone else
is allowing them to see our love towards
ourselves. Only through loving ourselves can we
feel love and compassion for someone else."
Barbara Lee (in Loving Yourself) proposes we
spend time each day breathing in the beauty of
who we are. (Numbers 40 – 45 are hers!)

41. "The reason someone else bothers you is because they remind you . . . of yourself. Treat your projections on others as a source of insight that reveals a hidden part of yourself. (But) please don't judge yourself, remember you are discovering your real self through this process."

42. "Go forth with an open heart, expecting this to be the most miraculous day of your life. "Whatever and whoever comes into your life . . is meant to be there." Life is unfolding and so are we. Pay attention to what is happening around you. Ask what importance new people or events contain for you.

43. How are you at forgiving?
When we learn to forgive, we
learn to heal. Judgments about us
can end. God is forgiving.
Shouldn't we be too?

44. Your life is your own movie - you
are the story-writer, the director, the
producer and the star. You have no one
to blame for the outcome of your movie.
Just experience, just feel, just be grateful
to be alive. The purpose of our
life/movie is to allow *Love* to enter, is to
allow love to soften your heart, and not
be afraid anymore."

45. Live your life as if today were the
first day of the last six months of your
life. Notice how this way of thinking
establishes much more clearly what is
really important to you. Notice how
people who have had a brush with death
or suffered a serious illness have clear
priorities.

Finding Personal Success

46. Play "Beach Bocce at least once in your life.
Read my book Beach Bocce Champion: Be A Winner!

47. Nobody knows the tips you need! Give yourself a tip that you know you need. You can write it in the space below.

Afterthoughts

Be a champion in your business!

This collection is a continuing project. You can participate in several ways, and two of them are to add your own wisdoms, or you can send them to me and I'll add them to the next edition. These came in chunks or at times when I thought either I had learned a new lesson or somebody like my friend Barbara Lee handed along their list. Some of my favorite authors are paraphrased here as well.

I'm a Psychologist and a Business Consultant, and I also have taught courses from each field. I see that there is great overlap. Everything I know about Psychology seems applicable to the business world in one way or another.

Some of these wisdoms are reworked from an optional assignment I gave to a Psychology class at Keiser University. Their task was to write tips they would pass along to their children. Recently, I had a community college client for whom I was building and managing a Leadership Series. Most of what I think they needed to learn is embodied here. I hope you enjoy this little book of wisdoms.

Doug Ross

Sarasota, FL
doug@doug-ross.com

Finding Personal Success

Who I am!

"I yam what I yam."
Popeye, The Sailor Man

In the last few weeks, I've been looking closely at my consulting business, and in a more general way, myself as a person. A visit by an old friend helped. My business groups have helped. My Mastermind group meets twice a month and we help each other with business challenges, some of which are pretty personal. At the YES group, I hear speakers talk about all the ways they became successful, and often that includes becoming aware of why some things failed. I compare myself.

My Networking Group that meets every week requires that I stand up and say what I do in a 30 second elevator speech. I keep refining it, and more and more see that success for me comes from knowing potential clients well and them knowing me well and trusting me. My groups exploring what we know about the brain as we age and the challenges of aging extends the reason to understand myself better too. In fact, when I look back at my working life, I think most of my success has come from knowing me well enough to also be sensitive to others. Only lately have I also seen that this sensitivity comes from being involved with associates and friends in ways that allow us to really get to know each other well, and the result is I know who the friends are that I like to be with and who I don't want to spend any time with if possible. I don't have to think or plan about this; it is what I do, what I am.

My Internet Marketing Mastermind group has caused me to think about marketing myself on my web sites, or in social media. I don't like to market myself or sell myself, and I am not good at it. I strongly prefer to meet with my friends person to person, and not via the internet or email, though I do keep in touch with my friends using email, but without person to person, it stays pretty shallow.

However, these experts show how to be successful and make good money on the internet using social media and jazzy web sites with videos and ways to opt in and get addresses, etc. I can't fully buy in. It just doesn't work for me.

I read an article about how trust and wisdom are often enhanced as people age, and it resonates with me. My best bet to get good work is to be interested enough in people that they like and trust me. So I had an "aha!" moment this week that in all the following kinds of interactions, being myself and asking questions that get people to share who they are and what they think is the best way to market my skills. It has been there for me as a student, as a father, as a husband, as a professor, in leadership roles I have had, in sports, in coaching, and in being a "soft leader" in the many groups I have been in or founded. My consulting style is called process consulting. It is knowing *how* people can be more successful, and helping them get to where they want to be. Much of knowing how to help is knowing who they are and knowing what I can contribute, i.e., knowing myself. [And that is the title of this book I think is my best effort, "Finding Personal Success: Knowing Yourself".]

In the "aha" experience I mentioned, I realized that I have learned much about myself and others, and among all those ways, a big chunk came from learning, teaching others, and practicing dialogue. [That is summarized in "The Tao of Dialogue".] Finally, now, at this stage in my 75 years of life, it is almost automatic for me. I ask people I meet and like a lot of questions about themselves, and I then listen without interrupting them. I realize that I can, by listening, as we used to say in dialogues, "walk in the other person's moccasins". I find I know what they are thinking and how they think and feel. I am automatically sensitive to their emotions. I can feel what they feel and I understand it. I do this, again automatically, with my extended family, grandchildren, and with all my sons.

75

Finding Personal Success

Stepping back from myself to get perspective, and my Mastermind Group friends help with this, I see knowing myself as my greatest strength. It isn't anything I can market or sell, all I can do is just be who I am and not question it. The only slight downside I can see so far is that I quickly pick up on phonies, on insensitive people, and on people not to be trusted. I seem to be better and am getting better at avoiding these types.

"I'm Popeye the sailor man,
I'm Popeye the sailor man.
I'm strong to the fin-ich
'Cause I eats my spin-ach
I'm Popeye the sailor man.

DAR
3/2023/2014

www.ingramcontent.com/pod-product-compliance
Lightning Source LLC
Chambersburg PA
CBHW021241280526
45784CB00005B/2188